弟 子 規

Standards for Students

Instructions in Virtue from the
Chinese Heritage

弟子規
Standards for Students:
Instructions in Virtue from the Chinese Heritage

Illustrations by: Soh-Hwa Liung and Ming-Hong Lim

Published and translated by:
Buddhist Text Translation Society
1777 Murchison Drive
Burlingame, California 94010-4504

©2010
Buddhist Text Translation Society
Instilling Goodness Elementary School
Dharma Realm Buddhist Association

First edition 2003
16 15 14 13 12 11   10 9 8 7 6 5 4 3 2

Printed in Taiwan, R.O.C.

Library of Congress Cataloging-in-Publication Data

Di zi gui. English
   Standards for students : instructions in virtue from the Chinese heritage = [Di zi gui] /
   translated by the Buddhist Text Translation Society.
        p. cm.
   Parallel title in Chinese characters.
   Chinese and English.
   Summary: Presents traditional Chinese (Confucian) teachings in verses which address
how to be careful and honest, cherish all beings, draw near to good people, and practice
other virtues.
   ISBN 978-0-88139-489-4
   1. Conduct of life--Juvenile literature. 2. Chinese language--Readers--Juvenile
literature. [Conduct of life. 2. Confucianism. 3. Chinese language
materials--Bilingual.] I. Title: Di zi gui. II. Buddhist Text Translation Society. III. Title.

BJ1588.C5 D52913 2003
170'.83--dc21

慈祥代天宣化
忠孝為國教民

According with Higher Goodness,
Proclaim and Transform with Kindness.
For the Sake of the Country,
Teach People to Be Loyal and Filial.

目錄
mù lù

Table of Contents

總敍
zǒng xù
Preface..1

第一章　入則孝
dì yī zhāng　rù zé xiào
Chapter 1　On Being Filial at Home....................3

第二章　出則弟
dì èr zhāng　chū zé tì
Chapter 2　On Practicing True Brotherhood........9

第三章　謹
dì sān zhāng　jǐn
Chapter 3　On Being Careful.................................15

第四章　信
dì sì zhāng　xìn
Chapter 4　On Being Honest.................................23

第五章　汎愛眾
dì wǔ zhāng　fàn ài zhòng
Chapter 5　On Cherishing All Living Beings.........29

第六章　親仁
dì liù zhāng　qīn rén
Chapter 6　On Drawing Near to Goodhearted
People...35

第七章　餘力學文
dì qī zhāng　yú lì xué wén
Chapter 7　On Studying Whenever We Can........37

弟子規者，弟子為學做人，待人處世之準繩也。

The *Standards for Students* are basic requisites for being a good person
and guidelines for living in harmony with others.

總ㄗㄨㄥˇ 敘ㄒㄩˋ
zǒng   xù

Preface

弟_{ㄉ一ˋ}子_{ㄗˇ}規_{ㄍㄨㄟ}　聖_{ㄕㄥˋ}人_{ㄖㄣˊ}訓_{ㄒㄩㄣˋ}　首_{ㄕㄡˇ}孝_{ㄒ一ㄠˋ}弟_{ㄊ一ˋ}　次_{ㄘˋ}謹_{ㄐ一ㄣˇ}信_{ㄒ一ㄣˋ}

dì　zǐ　guī　　shèng rén　xùn　　shǒu xiào tì　　cì　jǐn　xìn

These are the rules for being a student
Handed down to us by Ancient Sages.
First be filial to your own parents
And respectful to all of your elders.

汎_{ㄈㄢˋ}愛_{ㄞˋ}眾_{ㄓㄨㄥˋ}　而_{ㄦˊ}親_{ㄑ一ㄣ}仁_{ㄖㄣˊ}　有_{一ㄡˇ}餘_{ㄩˊ}力_{ㄌ一ˋ}　則_{ㄗㄜˊ}學_{ㄒㄩㄝˊ}文_{ㄨㄣˊ}

fàn　ài　zhòng　　ér　qīn　rén　　yǒu　yú　lì　　zé　xué　wén

Be trustworthy, cautious and kind,
And draw near to those who are good.
Whatever time you have left
Should be devoted to learning.

孝順子弟，善體親心，勞而不怨。

A filial child is considerate of his or her parents
and enthusiastically helps with the household chores.

第一章 入則孝
dì yī zhāng   rù   zé   xiào

Chapter 1
On Being Filial at Home

父母呼　應勿緩　父母命　行勿懶
fù mǔ hū　yìng wù huǎn　fù mǔ mìng　xíng wù lǎn

When your mother or father is calling,
Do not be slow to respond.
When your parents tell you to do something,
Do not be lazy or sulky.

父母教　須敬聽　父母責　須順承
fù mǔ jiāo　xū jìng tīng　fù mǔ zé　xū shùn chéng

When your parents need to instruct you,
You should listen with patient respect.
Whenever your parents must scold you,
Accept it with faithful compliance.

冬則溫　夏則清　晨則省　昏則定
dōng zé wēn　xià zé jìng　chén zé xǐng　hūn zé dìng

In the winter, make sure they are warm.
In the summer, make sure they are cool.
In the morning, cheerfully greet them.
In the evening, tell them "Good night."

出必告　反必面　居有常　業無變
chū bì gù　fǎn bì miàn　jū yǒu cháng　yè wú biàn

If you plan to go out, tell your parents.
Report to them when you get back.
Settle down in one certain place.
Do not switch from one job to another.

父母教導，恭敬承聽，不敢拂逆。
Respectfully listen to parents' guidance and instructions.

事雖小　勿擅爲　苟擅爲　子道虧
shì suī xiǎo　wù shàn wéi　gǒu shàn wéi　zǐ dào kuī

No matter how small the affair,
Do not act just as you please.
For if you act just as you please,
Then you have not performed as you should.

物雖小　勿私藏　苟私藏　親心傷
wù suī xiǎo　wù sī cáng　gǒu sī cáng　qīn xīn shāng

Although a thing may be small,
Do not save it just for yourself.
For if you hoard things for yourself,
Your parents' hearts will be grieved.

親所好　力爲具　親所惡　謹爲去
qīn suǒ hào　lì wèi jù　qīn sǔo wù　jǐn wèi qù

Whatever your parents like best,
You should provide for them soon.
Whatever your parents dislike,
You should do your best to remove.

身有傷　貽親憂　德有傷　貽親羞
shēn yǒu shāng　yí qīn yōu　dé yǒu shāng　yí qīn xiū

If you carelessly injure your body,
Your parents will worry and fret.
If you heedlessly damage your virtue,
You bring shame and disgrace to your parents.

親愛我　孝何難　親憎我　孝方賢
qīn ài wǒ　xiào hé nán　qīn zēng wǒ　xiào fāng xián

When your parents are loving and kind,
Of course it's not hard to be filial.
The true test of being a person
Comes when parents are hateful and cruel.

親有過　諫使更　怡吾色　柔吾聲
qīn yǒu guò　jiàn shǐ gēng　yí wú sè　róu wú shēng

If you recognize faults in your parents,
Exhort them to change for the better.
Speak to them kindly and gently
With a pleasant smile on your face.

和顏規過，父母不從，號泣復諫，又敬　　　　　　　不違。

If parents have faults, use kind and sincere words to exhort them to change.

諫ㄐㄧㄢ　不ㄅㄨ　入ㄖㄨ　悅ㄩㄝ　復ㄈㄨ　諫ㄐㄧㄢ　號ㄏㄠ　泣ㄑㄧ　隨ㄙㄨㄟ　撻ㄊㄚ　無ㄨ　怨ㄩㄢ

jiàn　bú　rù　　yuè　fù　jiàn　　háo　qì　suí　　tà　wú　yuàn

If they cannot accept your advice,
Wait for an opportune time.
You may even use tears to exhort them,
But don't resent it if you are punished.

親ㄑㄧㄣ　有ㄧㄡ　疾ㄐㄧ　藥ㄧㄠ　先ㄒㄧㄢ　嘗ㄔㄤ　晝ㄓㄡ　夜ㄧㄝ　侍ㄕ　不ㄅㄨ　離ㄌㄧ　床ㄔㄨㄤ

qīn　yǒu　jí　　yào　xiān　cháng　　zhòu　yè　shì　　bù　lí　chuáng

When your parents are ill, call the doctor,
Be sure the prescription is right.
Wait on them day after day,
At their bedside by day and by night.

喪三年　常悲咽　居處變　酒肉絕

sāng sān nián　cháng bēi yiè　jū chù biàn　jiǔ ròu jué

For three years after their death,
Remember them always in sorrow.
During this period of mourning,
Don't drink wine or eat meat.

喪盡禮　祭盡誠　事死者　如事生

sāng jìn lǐ　jì jìn chéng　shì sǐ zhě　rú shì shēng

Take care of their funeral arrangements,
Make offerings on their behalf.
Reverently cherish their memory
As if they were still in the world.

兄友弟恭，家庭和睦，百事呈祥。

When elder siblings treat younger siblings as friends,
and younger siblings respect their elder brothers and sisters,
the family is peaceful and happy.

第 dì 二 èr 章 zhāng　出 chū 則 zé 弟 tì

Chapter 2
On Practicing
True Brotherhood

兄道友　弟道恭　兄弟睦　孝在中

xiōng dào yǒu　dì dào gōng　xiōng dì mù　xiào zài zhōng

When the older children are friendly
And the younger children respectful,
Then brothers and sisters won't fight,
And it's clear they know how to be filial.

財物輕　怨何生　言語忍　忿自泯

cái wù qīng　yuàn hé shēng　yán yǔ rěn　fèn zì mǐn

Don't think of wealth as important,
Or else you will feel resentful.
When talking to others, be patient,
Then you won't be troubled by anger.

或飲食　或坐走　長者先　幼者後

huò yǐn shí　huò zuò zǒu　zhǎng zhě xiān　yòu zhě hòu

When people are eating or drinking,
Sitting down or taking a walk,
Let those who are older go first.
The young ones should follow behind.

長呼人　即代叫　人不在　己即到

zhǎng hū rén　jí dài jiào　rén bú zài　jǐ jí dào

If an elder is looking for someone,
You should run the errand instead.
If the person you seek can't be found,
Hurry back and report what you've learned.

兄弟姊妹，互相切磋，其樂融融。

When brothers and sisters study together,
a harmonious atmosphere is created.

稱尊長　勿呼名　對尊長　勿見能

chēng zūn zhǎng　　wù hū míng　　duì zūn zhǎng　　wù xiàn néng

In speaking to those who are older,
Use the proper terms of respect.
When you are facing teachers and elders,
Don't show off or try to look smart.

路遇長　疾趨揖　長無言　退恭立

lù yù zhǎng　　jí qū yī　　zhǎng wú yán　　tuì gōng lì

If you meet an elder while walking,
Greet him or her with respect.
If the elder does not address you,
Respectfully stand to one side.

騎下馬　乘下車　過猶待　百步餘
qí xià mǎ　chéng xià jū　guò yóu dài　bǎi bù yú

If an elder's walking and you're riding,
Stop and ask if he's traveling far.
Respectfully wait till he's passed you
Before you continue on in your car.

長者立　幼勿坐　長者坐　命乃坐
zhǎng zhě lì　yòu wù zuò　zhǎng zhě zuò　mìng nǎi zuò

When an elder person is standing,
The young ones should not take a seat,
But wait till the elder is seated,
And sit down when you are told.

尊長前　聲要低　低不聞　卻非宜
zūn zhǎng qián　shēng yào dī　dī bù wén　què fēi yí

Speak softly in front of your elders,
In a low voice that pleases the ear.
But you are wrong if you're speaking
So softly that no one can hear.

進必趨　退必遲　問起對　視勿移
jìn bì qū　tuì bì chí　wèn qǐ duì　shì wù yí

Greet your elders promptly,
And take your leave slowly.
Answer questions respectfully,
And don't let your eyes dart around.

飲食坐走，長幼有序，不失禮節。

When walking, sitting, or eating, there should always be a certain order;
those who are younger usually let the elders go first.

事 諸 父 如 事 父 事 諸 兄 如 事 兄
shì zhū fù   rú shì fù   shì zhū xiōng   rú shì xiōng

You should treat everyone's parents
Just the same as you treat your own.
Treat all brothers and sisters
Just like your family at home.

言行舉止，謹慎小心，無過安然。

In actions and speech, one should always be cautious and careful;
having no faults, one is safe and peaceful.

第三章　謹
dì　sān　zhāng　jǐn

Chapter 3
On Being Careful

朝_{ㄓㄠ} 起_{ㄑㄧ} 早_{ㄗㄠ}　夜_{ㄧㄝ} 眠_{ㄇㄧㄢ} 遲_ㄔ　老_{ㄌㄠ} 易_ㄧ 至_ㄓ　惜_{ㄒㄧ} 此_ㄘ 時_ㄕ

zhāo　qǐ　zǎo　　yè　mián　chí　　lǎo　yì　zhì　　xí　cǐ　shí

In the morning it's best to rise early.
At night you should go to bed late.
Cherish the time that is left you.
Don't expect that old age will wait.

晨_{ㄔㄣ} 必_{ㄅㄧ} 盥_{ㄍㄨㄢ}　兼_{ㄐㄧㄢ} 漱_{ㄕㄨ} 口_{ㄎㄡ}　便_{ㄅㄧㄢ} 溺_{ㄋㄧㄠ} 回_{ㄏㄨㄟ}　輒_{ㄓㄜ} 淨_{ㄐㄧㄥ} 手_{ㄕㄡ}

chén　bì　quàn　　jiān　shù　kǒu　　biàn　niào　húi　　zhé　jìng　shǒu

In the morning, first wash your face,
And next brush your teeth very well.
After you go to the toilet,
Use water and soap on your hands.

冠_{ㄍㄨㄢ} 必_{ㄅㄧ} 正_{ㄓㄥ}　紐_{ㄋㄧㄡ} 必_{ㄅㄧ} 結_{ㄐㄧㄝ}　襪_{ㄨㄚ} 與_ㄩ 履_{ㄌㄩ}　俱_{ㄐㄩ} 緊_{ㄐㄧㄣ} 切_{ㄑㄧㄝ}

guān　bì　zhèng　　niǔ　bì　jié　　wà　yǔ　lǚ　　jù　jǐn　qiè

You should put on your hat with care,
And fasten your buttons and snaps.
Then pull up your socks very neatly,
And fasten your shoelaces as well.

置_ㄓ 冠_{ㄍㄨㄢ} 服_{ㄈㄨ}　有_{ㄧㄡ} 定_{ㄉㄧㄥ} 位_{ㄨㄟ}　勿_ㄨ 亂_{ㄌㄨㄢ} 頓_{ㄉㄨㄣ}　致_ㄓ 污_ㄨ 穢_{ㄏㄨㄟ}

zhì　guān　fú　　yǒu　dìng　wèi　　wù　luàn　dùn　　zhì　wū　huì

Your hat and other clothes
Should be put in their own special places.
Do not leave them just lying around,
Or they're sure to get wrinkled and soiled.

飲食簡約，衣不貴華，勤儉自持。

Eat simple food and wear simple clothes; always try to be frugal.

衣 yī 貴 guì 潔 jié　不 bú 貴 guì 華 húa　上 shàng 循 xún 分 fèn　下 xià 稱 chèn 家 jiā

Your clothing should always be neat.
If it's not new and stylish, don't worry.
What you wear should make common sense.
Don't spend too much money on clothes.

對 duì 飲 yǐn 食 shí　勿 wù 揀 jiǎn 擇 zé　食 shí 適 shì 可 kě　勿 wù 過 guò 則 zé

Do not fuss and complain about tastes
When you are given something to eat.
Eat enough so that you are full,
But do not eat more than you need.

17

年方少 少 勿飲酒 飲酒醉 最爲醜
nián fāng shào　wù yǐn jiǔ　yǐn jiǔ zuì　zuì wéi chǒu

During the time when you are young,
Don't drink liquor or take harmful drugs.
To get drunk is disgraceful and ugly.
Taking drugs brings you nothing but shame.

步從容 立端正 揖深圓 拜恭敬
bù cōng róng　lì duān zhèng　yī shēn yuán　bài gōng jìng

Your walk should be easy and graceful.
When you stand, keep your back tall and straight.
Your half bows should be deep and full,
And your full bows made with respect.

勿踐閾 勿跛倚 勿箕踞 勿搖髀
wù jiàn yù　wù bì yǐ　wù jī jù　wù yáo bì

Watch your step as you enter a doorway.
Stand up straight and don't lean against the wall.
Do not sit sprawled all over the floor.
Or wriggle and squirm when you walk.

緩揭簾 勿有聲 寬轉彎 勿觸棱
huǎn jiē lián　wù yǒu shēng　kuān zhuǎn wān　wù chù léng

When closing a door best be careful,
Do it slowly without too much noise.
Whenever crossing a room,
Don't bump into the table and chairs.

行步從容，舉止端莊，不緩不躁。

Be graceful in every movement.
When walking, standing or sitting down, don't move too fast or too slow.

執 虛 器 　 如 執 盈 　 入 虛 室 　 如 有 人
zhí xū qì 　 rú zhí yíng 　 rù xū shì 　 rú yǒu rén

You should carry an empty container,
Just as carefully as one that is full.
And enter a room that is empty,
As you would if a crowd were inside.

事 勿 忙 　 忙 多 錯 　 勿 畏 難 　 勿 輕 略
shì wù máng 　 máng duō cuò 　 wù wèi nán 　 wù qīng lüè

There is no need to be in a hurry.
If you rush you will make a mistake.
Don't be afraid of what's hard,
And don't be careless with what is easy.

鬥鬧場 絕勿近 邪僻事 絕勿問
dòu nào chǎng   jué wù jìn   xié pì shì   jué wù wèn

Never go to rowdy places,
Or places where people are fighting.
When something is low and improper
It's not worth your talk or your questions.

將入門 問孰存 將上堂 聲必揚
jiāng rù mén   wèn shú cún   jiāng shàng táng   shēng bì yáng

When you're going to enter a room,
First knock to make sure it's permitted.
When joining a gathering of people,
Let them all know you've arrived.

人問誰 對以名 吾與我 不分明
rén wèn shuí   duì yǐ míng   wú yǔ wǒ   bù fēn míng

If someone should ask who you are,
You should answer by giving your name.
If you respond, "It is me,"
You're not giving a proper reply.

用人物 須明求 倘不問 即為偷
yòng rén wù   xū míng qiú   tǎng bú wèn   jí wéi tōu

If you use someone else's belongings,
Be sure that you ask for permission.
If you don't get the owner's permission,
Then stealing is what you have done.

鬥鬧市井，邪僻惡友，應當遠離。

Keep far away from places where people are fighting,
and avoid making bad friends.

借_{ㄐㄧㄝ}人_{ㄖㄣ}物_ㄨ 及_{ㄐㄧ}時_ㄕ還_{ㄏㄨㄢ} 後_{ㄏㄡ}有_{ㄧㄡ}急_{ㄐㄧ} 借_{ㄐㄧㄝ}不_{ㄅㄨ}難_{ㄋㄢ}

jiè rén wù   jí shí huán   hòu yǒu jí   jiè bù nán

If you must borrow something from another,
Make sure you return it on time.
If someone asks you for something,
Loan it to them as soon as you can.

言語誠信，行為篤敬，以德自勵。

Be honest and trustworthy in words and behavior.
And make developing virtue a top priority.

第勹四公章业尤　信丁与
dì　sì　zhāng　xìn

Chapter 4
On Being Honest

凡 出 言 信 爲 先 詐 與 妄 奚 可 焉
fán chū yán   xìn wéi xiān   zhà yǔ wàng   xī kě yān

Whatever it is that you say,
You should speak so that you can be trusted.
Tell the truth so others can believe you.
To lie is against human nature.

話 説 多 不 如 少 惟 其 是 勿 佞 巧
huà shuō duō   bù rú shǎo   wéi qí shì   wù nìng qiǎo

To talk just a little is better
Than to chatter non-stop all day long.
Talk only about what you're sure of;
Avoid cunning or flowery words.

奸 巧 語 穢 污 詞 市 井 氣 切 戒 之
jiān qiǎo yǔ   huì wū cí   shì jǐng qì   qiè jiè zhī

Don't use words to be mean and cruel,
Or speak about things that are coarse.
Let your language be pure and correct.
Stay away from all that's unworthy.

見 未 眞 勿 輕 言 知 未 的 勿 輕 傳
jiàn wèi zhēn   wù qīng yán   zhī wèi dì   wù qīng chuán

If you haven't seen something quite clearly,
Don't speak of it as if you know.
If you're not sure about what exactly happened,
Don't spread rumors around.

穢污之詞，佞巧之語，人所惡聞。

Swear words, cunning phrases, and flowery speech are not nice to hear.

事ㄕ 非ㄈㄟ 宜ㄧ 勿ㄨ 輕ㄑㄧㄥ 諾ㄋㄨㄛ 苟ㄍㄡ 輕ㄑㄧㄥ 諾ㄋㄨㄛ 進ㄐㄧㄣ 退ㄊㄨㄟ 錯ㄘㄨㄛ

shì   fēi   yí   wù   qīng   nuò   gǒu   qīng   nuò   jìn   tuì   cuò

When you know something is wrong,
Do not simply follow along.
If you just go along with the crowd,
You're bound to make a mistake.

凡ㄈㄢ 道ㄉㄠ 字ㄗ 重ㄓㄨㄥ 且ㄑㄧㄝ 舒ㄕㄨ 勿ㄨ 急ㄐㄧ 疾ㄐㄧ 勿ㄨ 模ㄇㄛ 糊ㄏㄨ

fán   dào   zì   zhòng   qiě   shū   wù   jí   jí   wù   mó   hú

When you speak, say the words clearly;
Distinctly and smoothly they flow.
If you talk too fast, no one will heed you;
The same if you mumble too low.

彼說長　此說短　不關己　莫閒管

bǐ shuō cháng　cǐ shūo duǎn　bù quān jǐ　mò xián guǎn

Some like to talk about good points,
Others like to find faults, big and small.
If something is none of your business,
Simply pay no attention at all.

見人善　即思齊　縱去遠　以漸躋

jiàn rén shàn　jí sī qí　zòng qù yuǎn　yǐ jiàn jī

When you see the good points of others,
You should strive to imitate them.
Though you don't match up to them now,
Persevere and one day you'll catch up.

見人惡　即內省　有則改　無加警

jiàn rén è　jí nèi xǐng　yǒu zé gǎi　wú jiā jǐng

When you notice bad habits in others,
Reflect on your own shortcomings.
If you have the same faults, correct them.
If not, never let them arise.

唯德學　唯才藝　不如人　當自礪

wéi dé xué　wéi cái yì　bù rú rén　dāng zì lì

If your virtue, learning and talents
Don't measure up to others,
Then spur yourself to work harder.
Accept nothing less than your best.

歡喜納諫，惡友遠離，益友相親。

If one can appreciate the value of criticism,
bad friends will stay away and wholesome friends will draw near.

若衣服　若飲食　不如人　勿生慼
ruò yī fú　ruò yǐn shí　bù rú rén　wù shēng qī

If your wardrobe is seldom in fashion
And your home is simple and plain,
While your friends have the newest and finest,
Don't be upset and never complain.

聞過怒　聞譽樂　損友來　益友卻
wén guò nù　wén yù lè　sǔn yǒu lái　yì yǒu què

If you're angry when told of your faults,
And happy when praise comes your way,
Harmful friends will draw near you,
And wholesome friends will stay away.

聞ㄨㄣˊ 譽ㄩˋ 恐ㄎㄨㄥˇ　聞ㄨㄣˊ 過ㄍㄨㄛˋ 欣ㄒㄧㄣ　直ㄓˊ 諒ㄌㄧㄤˋ 士ㄕˋ　漸ㄐㄧㄢˋ 相ㄒㄧㄤ 親ㄑㄧㄣ

wén　yù　kǒng　　wén　guò　xīn　　zhí　liàng　shì　　jiàn　xiāng　qīn

If compliments make you uneasy
And hearing your faults makes you glad,
Forgiving and straightforward friends
Will then gradually come to your side.

無ㄨˊ 心ㄒㄧㄣ 非ㄈㄟ　名ㄇㄧㄥˊ 爲ㄨㄟˊ 錯ㄘㄨㄛˋ　有ㄧㄡˇ 心ㄒㄧㄣ 非ㄈㄟ　名ㄇㄧㄥˊ 爲ㄨㄟˊ 惡ㄜˋ

wú　xīn　fēi　　míng　wéi　cuò　　yǒu　xīn　fēi　　míng　wéi　è

When an error is not made on purpose,
It is simply called a mistake.
But to deliberately do something wrong,
Is not a mistake, but an evil.

過ㄍㄨㄛˋ 能ㄋㄥˊ 改ㄍㄞˇ　歸ㄍㄨㄟ 於ㄩˊ 無ㄨˊ　倘ㄊㄤˇ 掩ㄧㄢˇ 飾ㄕˋ　增ㄗㄥ 一ㄧˋ 辜ㄍㄨ

guò　néng　gǎi　　gūi　yú　wú　　tǎng　yǎn　shì　　zēng　yì　gū

If you can reform your offenses,
Your faults will all disappear.
But trying to cover them over
Makes your offenses more severe.

天地平等覆育萬物，應加愛惜。

Mother nature nurtures living creatures without discrimination.
Everyone should cherish each other's right to live.

第 ㄉㄧˋ 五 ㄨˇ 章 ㄓㄤ　　汎 ㄈㄢˋ 愛 ㄞˋ 眾 ㄓㄨㄥˋ
dì　wǔ　zhāng　　fàn　ài　zhòng

Chapter 5
On Cherishing
All Living Beings

凡是人　皆須愛　天同覆　地同載

fán shì rén　jiē xū ài　tiān tóng fù　dì tóng zài

For all creatures throughout the world,
One should cherish a kind regard.
The sky covers all of us equally.
The earth supports all humankind.

行高者　名自高　人所重　非貌高

xìng gāo zhě　míng zì gāo　rén suǒ chòng　fēi mào gāo

People whose conduct is fine
Are sure to have good reputations.
Good conduct is what we respect;
Fine looks cannot bring people honor.

才大者　望自大　人所服　非言大

cái dà zhě　wàng zì dà　rén suǒ fú　fēi yán dà

People who have great ability
Thereby enjoy great prestige.
Others will follow their lead,
But great talkers don't earn much respect.

己有能　勿自私　人所能　勿輕訾

jǐ yǒu néng　wù zì sī　rén suǒ néng　wù qīng zǐ

The abilities you yourself have
Should not be used to attain selfish goals.
The abilities others may have
Should not be belittled and scorned.

見人貧困，孤苦無依，應溫恤救濟。

Help the needy, comfort the lonely, and encourage those in difficulty.

勿諂富　勿驕貧　勿厭故　勿喜新
wù chǎn fù　wù jiāo pín　wù yàn gù　wù xǐ xīn

It's not right to flatter the rich
Or be arrogant towards the poor.
What's old need not be rejected.
What's new is not necessarily good.

人不閒　勿事攪　人不安　勿話擾
rén bù xián　wù shì jiǎo　rén bù ān　wù huà rǎo

If you see a person who's busy,
Leave him alone until he's free.
If you see that a person is upset,
Don't annoy him with idle chatter.

31

人 有 短　切 莫 揭　人 有 私　切 莫 説
rén yǒu duǎn　qiè mò jiē　rén yǒu sī　qiè mò shuō

Although you may know someone's faults,
There's no need to tell everyone.
The personal business of others
Should not be the subject of talk.

道 人 善　即 是 善　人 知 之　愈 思 勉
dào rén shàn　jí shì shàn　rén zhī zhī　yù sì miǎn

Praising the virtue of others
Is itself a virtuous deed.
When people hear they've been praised,
They will want to improve even more.

揚 人 惡　即 是 惡　疾 之 甚　禍 且 作
yáng rén è　jí shì è　jí zhī shèn　huò qiě zuò

There is never anything good
In talking of others' shortcomings.
If they hear, they will surely resent it;
They will see you mean nothing but trouble.

善 相 勸　德 皆 建　過 不 規　道 兩 虧
shàn xiāng quàn　dé jiē jiàn　guò bù guī　dào liǎng kuī

We should urge each other towards goodness
And develop our virtue together.
If our faults are not corrected,
We will surely stray from the Way.

見人為善，隨喜讚歎，人愈思勉。

Praise those who do good works; they will be encouraged to continue.

凡ㄈㄢˊ 取ㄑㄩˇ 與ㄩˇ　貴ㄍㄨㄟˋ 分ㄈㄣ 曉ㄒㄧㄠˇ　與ㄩˇ 宜ㄧˊ 多ㄉㄨㄛ　取ㄑㄩˇ 宜ㄧˊ 少ㄕㄠˇ

fán qǔ yǔ　guì fēn xiǎo　yǔ yí duō　qǔ yí shǎo

The amount you give and you get
Should always be clearly distinguished.
Make sure that your giving surpasses
The amount that you receive.

將ㄐㄧㄤ 加ㄐㄧㄚ 人ㄖㄣˊ　先ㄒㄧㄢ 問ㄨㄣˋ 己ㄐㄧˇ　己ㄐㄧˇ 不ㄅㄨˋ 欲ㄩˋ　即ㄐㄧˊ 速ㄙㄨˋ 已ㄧˇ

jiāng jiā rén　xiān wèn jǐ　jǐ bú yù　jí sù yǐ

Before you begin to blame others,
First you should question yourself:
"Would I want to be scolded and blamed?"
If not, then don't do it to someone else.

恩ㄣ 欲ㄩ 報ㄠ　怨ㄩㄢ 欲ㄩ 忘ㄨㄤ　報ㄠ 怨ㄩㄢ 短ㄉㄨㄢ　報ㄠ 恩ㄣ 長ㄔㄤ

ēn　yù　bào　　yuàn　yù　wáng　　bào　yuàn　duǎn　　bào　ēn　cháng

Kindness must be returned.
Let enmity just fade away.
Grudges are better forgotten;
Make kindness increase day by day.

待ㄉㄞ 婢ㄅㄧ 僕ㄆㄨ　身ㄕㄣ 貴ㄍㄨㄟ 端ㄉㄨㄢ　雖ㄙㄨㄟ 貴ㄍㄨㄟ 端ㄉㄨㄢ　慈ㄘ 而ㄦ 寬ㄎㄨㄢ

dài　bì　pú　　shēn　quì　duān　　suī　quì　duān　　cí　ér　kuān

Treat your employees with fairness.
Be proper and just with each one.
And not only proper and just--
You should also be kind and forgiving.

勢ㄕ 服ㄈㄨ 人ㄖㄣ　心ㄒㄧㄣ 不ㄅㄨ 然ㄖㄢ　理ㄌㄧ 服ㄈㄨ 人ㄖㄣ　方ㄈㄤ 無ㄨ 言ㄧㄢ

shì　fú　rén　　xīn　bù　rán　　lǐ　fú　rén　　fāng　wú　yán

If you try to rule others by force,
You will never win over their hearts.
If you lead them with virtue and reason,
Then they won't feel oppressed and apart.

以善為寶，以仁為親，可躋聖賢。

By seeing goodness as a treasure and humaneness as a close friend,
one can reach the level of sages.

第六章　親仁
dì　liù　zhāng　qīn　rén

Chapter 6
On Drawing Near to
Goodhearted People

同是人　類不齊　流俗眾　仁者希
tóng shì rén　lèi bù qí　liú sú zhòng　rén zhě xī

Many different kinds of people
All live on the earth together.
There are many who follow the crowd.
There are few who are truly humane.

果仁者　人多畏　言不諱　色不媚
guǒ rén zhě　rén duō wèi　yán bú huì　sè bú mèi

Yet those who are truly humane
Are often feared by other people,
For they don't hide behind words
Or try to please with their looks.

能親仁　無限好　德日進　過日少
néng qīn rén　wú xiàn hǎo　dé rì jìn　guò rì shǎo

To follow the truly humane
Will bring immeasurable good.
Virtue will grow day by day;
Mistakes will slowly fade away.

不親仁　無限害　小人進　百事壞
bù qīn rén　wú xiàn hài　xiǎo rén jìn　bǎi shì huài

Not to follow the truly humane
Will bring immeasurable harm,
Unworthy people will draw near you,
And everything will go awry.

廣學多聞，審問慎思，明辨篤行。

Diligently study to broaden your knowledge;
ask questions and think deeply about what you have learned.
Distinguish between right and wrong, and put what is right into practice.

第 dì　七 qī　章 zhāng　餘 yú　力 lì　學 xué　文 wén

Chapter 7
On Studying
Whenever We Can

不力行 但學文 長浮華 成何人
bú lì xíng　dàn xué wén　zhǎng fú huá　chéng hé rén

Cultural refinements have value,
But not at the expense of real work.
If you're just superficially polished,
Then what can you expect to become?

但力行 不學文 任己見 昧理眞
dàn lì xíng　bù xué wén　rèn jǐ jiàn　mèi lǐ zhēn

But if you do nothing but work
And have no understanding of culture,
You'll be bound by your own narrow views,
And your notions of truth will be murky.

讀書法 有三到 心眼口 信皆要
dú shū fǎ　yǒu sān dào　xīn yǎn kǒu　xìn jiē yào

When you're pursuing your studies,
On the "three places" focus attention:
Your mind, your eyes and your mouth.
It's important to train all these three.

方讀此 勿慕彼 此未終 彼勿起
fāng dú cǐ　wù mù bǐ　cǐ wèi zhōng　bǐ wù qǐ

When you've taken up study of something,
Don't let yourself become sidetracked.
Be sure that you've finished one project
Before starting off on another.

立身行道，進德修業，以顯揚父母。

Establish a foundation for being a good person,
follow the path of truth, be virtuous, and study diligently;
your parents will benefit from your excellence.

寬 爲 限　　緊 用 功　　工 夫 到　　滯 塞 通
kuān wéi xiàn　　jǐn yòng gōng　　gōng fū dào　　zhì sè tōng

Let your goals be lofty and broad.
Let your efforts be focused and steady.
Once you have skill and experience,
You'll solve every problem with ease.

心 有 疑　　隨 札 記　　就 人 問　　求 確 義
xīn yǒu yí　　suí zhá jì　　jiù rén wèn　　qiú què yì

When a question comes up in your reading,
Make note of it before you forget.
Then ask someone else who will know,
And who can explain the meaning.

房室清　牆壁淨　几案潔　筆硯正
fáng shì qīng　qiáng bì jìng　jǐ àn jié　bǐ yàn zhèng

Your room should be kept neat and tidy,
With walls and floors uncluttered and clean.
Your desk should be kept in good order,
Pencils, paper, and pens well arranged.

墨磨偏　心不端　字不敬　心先病
mò mó piān　xīn bù duān　zì bú jìng　xīn xiān bìng

If your desk and papers are messy,
It is likely your mind's mixed up too.
If your writing is sloppy and careless,
It's likely your mind is not focused.

列典籍　有定處　讀看畢　還原處
liè diǎn jí　yǒu dìng chù　dú kàn bì　huán yuán chù

Each of the books that you use
Should have its proper place on the shelf.
After you've finished your reading,
Put them back in the place they belong.

雖有急　卷束齊　有缺壞　就補之
sūi yǒu jí　juàn shù qí　yǒu quē huài　jiù bǔ zhī

Although you may be in a hurry,
You should close your books the right way.
If the pages or covers are damaged,
Be sure to take time to repair them.

CONFUCIUS   WASHINGTON

哲人日已遠，典型在夙昔；風簷展書讀，古道照顏色。

Although the ancient sages lived long ago,
they are worthy models for all generations.
The true principles of their teachings will always connect.

非 聖 書　　屏 勿 視　　蔽 聰 明　　壞 心 志
fēi shèng shū　　bǐng wù shì　　bì cōng míng　　huài xīn zhì

What hasn't been written by sages
Is not something you should be reading.
Such books block your intelligence
And undermine your resolve.

勿 自 暴　　勿 自 棄　　聖 與 賢　　可 馴 致
wù zì bào　　wù zì qì　　shèng yǔ xián　　kě xún zhì

Don't ever look down on yourself
Or fail to progress toward goodness.
We all can gradually learn
To become worthies and sages.

學之於身　行之於身
Learn It and Put It into Practice

宣化上人一九八八年十月二十五日開示
A Dharma Talk by the Venerable Master Hua on October 25, 1988

教育有八種條目。在孔夫子的《大學》裏頭講「三綱領」、「八條目」。三綱領就是「明明德，親民，止於至善」；八條目就是「格物、致知、誠意、正心、修身、齊家、治國、平天下」。這是一整套做人的方法，也是治家、治國的方法。若能教育學生把三綱領、八條目都學之於身，行之於身，那麼這樣教育下一代，就會令他們都不捨本逐末。

There are Eight Articles of education. The Great Learning of Confucius discusses the Three Principles and Eight Articles. The Three Principles are "to exhibit understanding and virtue, to renew the people, and to rest in the highest goodness." The Eight Articles are to get rid of desires, extend knowledge, make thoughts sincere, rectify the mind, cultivate oneself, regulate the family, govern the country, and bring peace to the world." This is a complete set of methods for being a person, managing a family and ruling a country. If we can educate the next generation of the world by letting all students study the Three Principles and Eight Articles and put them into practice, then they won't forget what's vital or pursue unimportant things.

現在一般的教育，教育學生只知道將書讀好後，怎樣去找一個高的職位，賺的錢多，及怎樣能做世界的名人、世界第一的人。這是你沒有教他基本做人的道理，就教他去爭名奪利，這叫捨本逐末，背道而馳，是大錯而特錯的。所以為人師表，應該注意學生的品德和智慧，要開啟他的智慧之源，令他把本有智慧的泉源發掘出來，必須要耐心地去教育。

The typical education nowadays only teaches students how to get a high position and make a lot of money, how to become famous, and how to be number one in the world after they graduate. Instead of teaching them the basic requirements for being a person, we teach them to contend for fame and profit. This is known as renouncing the root and grasping at branches: going against the Way. To do things against the Way is a great mistake. Therefore, teachers should serve as good role models and pay attention to students' integrity and wisdom. Help them discover their inherent wisdom. Be patient in educating them.

這個事情的責任是非常重大的，你若把學生都教育得人人知道愛護自己的身、自己的家、自己的國，那麼，你不求世界和平，它也和平了。因為人不給自己麻煩，也就不會給旁人麻煩。在家庭不做不合理的事情，那麼在團體裏也會做循規蹈矩的良好公民。在社會上也能影響一般人都是互相尊重，互相愛敬，不會互相欺騙，互相打妄語。

Education is an extremely important responsibility. If we can teach every student to cherish his body, his family, and his country, then even if we aren't seeking world peace, the world will become peaceful. Why? People will not make trouble for themselves or for others. They won't do irrational things at home and they will be good law-abiding citizens in the community. In the society they will influence people to honor and cherish one another, and not cheat or lie to one another.

這個地方我相信是很要緊的！但是一般人，現在都忽略這根本的問題，都往末梢上跑，跑來跑去，離做人的本份就越跑越遠！我今天本照我很沒有經驗、很沒有學識的話，對大家來講這一種很普通的道理，可說是白水熬白菜，淡而無味。雖然沒有什麼味道，但是你若吃了白菜和白菜湯，就能解去很多的毒氣！

I believe that these aspects of the education process are crucial. However, many people have ignored these fundamental issues and instead pursue superficial matters. Running here and there, they get farther and farther from their basic human obligations. I have very little experience and knowledge, but I am telling everyone a very ordinary principle. You may say it is as tasteless as cabbage boiled in plain water. Although there's not much flavor, if you eat the cabbage and drink the soup, it can neutralize a lot of toxic energy!

教育語錄
Quotations on Education
宣化上人開示
From the Venerable Master Hua's Lectures

◆ 要改變教育的風氣，為這個，我們辦教育。
The trends in education must be changed. That's why we are working on education.

◆ 我辦教育，不單續佛慧命，也是續眾生的慧命。我們把學校辦好了，將來學生出了校門，能懂得怎麼樣面對社會，就能影響全社會都改變風氣。
In organizing schools, I want to perpetuate both the wisdom of the Buddha and the wisdom of living beings. If we do a good job in our schools, then after the students graduate, they will know how to interact with society and exert a positive influence on it.

美國萬佛聖城育良小學、
培德中學、法界佛教大學創辦人——

宣化上人簡介：

A Brief Introduction to Venerable Master Hsuan Hua,

Founder of Instilling Goodness Elementary School, Developing Virtue Secondary School, and Dharma Realm Buddhist University at the City of Ten Thousand Buddhas

◆ 來自白雪皚皚的中國長白山區。十九歲出家修道，發願普渡一切眾生。一九六二年將正確真實的佛法，由東方帶到西方——美國，是在西方建立三寶的第一人。

The Master came from the snow-laden vicinity of Eternally White Mountains in northeastern China. At the age of nineteen, he became a Buddhist monk and vowed to save all living beings. In 1962 he brought the Proper Buddhadharma from East to West and established the Triple Jewel on American soil.

◆ 「我從虛空來，回到虛空去」（一九九五年圓寂），終其一生儘量幫助世界走向安樂光明的途徑，大慈悲普渡，流血汗，不休息！

In 1995 before passing into stillness, he said, "I came from empty space, and to empty space I will return." Throughout his life he promoted peace and light in the world, compassionately and tirelessly rescuing living beings.

◆ 教育理念：栽培品德高尚的有志青年，為人群謀幸福，為世界造和平，教導學子「明理」，非為「名利」。是故育良小學和培德中學的宗旨是「孝」、「忠」，教導學生愛身、愛家、愛國。法界大學則講「仁義道德」，要在世界做一個好人。

His philosophy of education: To nurture young people of high moral character and aspirations, who will work for the welfare of humanity and for world peace, we must teach students to understand principles, not to merely seek fame and profit. Thus Instilling Goodness Elementary School and Developing Virtue Secondary School promote filial piety and social responsibility, teaching students to cherish themselves and love their families and country. Dharma Realm Buddhist University focuses on humaneness, justice, and ethical virtue, and teaches students how to be good citizens of the world.

育良小學重孝道　身體力行化氣質

Instilling Goodness Elementary School emphasizes filial piety.
The practice of filial piety transforms students' characters.

一九七四年秋，宣公上人在三藩市國際譯經學院附設育良小學，提倡孝
道，教導兒童孝順父母、恭敬師長，灌輸正當的道德思想，以期望兒童
將來成為善良守法的好公民。

In the autumn of 1974, the Venerable Master established Instilling Goodness Elementary
School, which emphasizes filial piety, at the International Institute for the Translation of
Buddhist Texts in San Francisco. Wishing children to become good and law-abiding
citizens, the school instills proper moral values in studends, teaching them to be filial to
their parents and to respect teachers and elders.

育良小學於一九七六年，遷於萬佛聖城。分為男女兩校。訓練男女有別
的禮節，並鼓勵兒童專心學習，協助道場工作，養成明辨是非，為人類
服務的精神。

Instilling Goodness Elementary School moved to the City in 1976. Boys and girls study separately. Gender separation teaches children about decorum and helps them to concentrate on their studies and community work. Students learn to differentiate between right and wrong and aspire to help and serve humanity.

上人在未出家前，是位孝子，遠近聞名。因此，育良小學也以灌注濃厚的道德思想及孝順父母為該校箴規。《弟子規》與《三字經》的中英文版本是學生必須熟讀的教材，這些為人處事的道理，播種在兒童心中，將來必能產生潛移默化的效果。

Before the Venerable Master became a monk, he was widely known as a filial son. Therefore, Instilling Goodness Elementary School also emphasizes virtue and filiality in its mission. Students are required to study *The Standards for Students* and the *The Three Character Classic* in Chinese and English. Like seeds planted in children's hearts, these principles of basic human morality and social etiquette will imperceptibly exert a positive influence on their future.

現代許多兒童，小小年紀便受電視、錄影帶、電影、光碟、電動遊戲中情慾、暴力等情節所影響，令為人父母者憂心不已。育良小學提供的純淨環境和中英雙語教學，因此不僅吸引了附近社區──瑜伽市的學生來此就讀，甚至美國加州及世界各地亦有學生前來。

Nowadays, parents are extremely concerned because children from a very young age are exposed to and affected by the sex and violence they see on television and in videos, movies, CDs, and video games. Instilling Goodness Elementary School, however, provides a pure and safe environment plus Chinese and English bilingual education. The diverse student body includes not only students from the local Ukiah community, but also students from other parts of California, the United States, and the world.

教師——
必須隨時成長
Teachers
Should Continually
Learn and Grow

王培榮/文
by Huang Pei-rong

當一般教師在教學時，往往把兒童看做一種容器，只等著用各種知識與經驗去裝滿。教師們並不明白兒童必須發展自己生命潛能的真相。

When ordinary teachers teach, they usually treat children as if they were some sort of container just waiting to be filled with all kinds of knowledge and experience. They ignore the fact that children need to develop the potential of their own lives.

事實上，教師必須預備一個符合兒童內在需求的「適當」環境，以充分發揮潛能。教師應當知道如何準備一個生動、活潑的環境，教師是兒童與環境之間的「有力聯繫」，一個教師的工作便是建立起環境與兒童心智的聯繫。教師在兒童學習環境中是一個主要成員。

In fact, teachers ought to prepare a "suitable" environment which fits the children's developmental needs so that their learning potential can be fully developed. Teachers should know how to prepare a vital and lively environment. A teacher is the "active link" between children and the surrounding environment. A teacher's job is to establish contacts between the surrounding environment and the children's minds. Teachers are a major element in the children's learning environment.

所以，教師必須經過訓
練，因為並不是單用邏輯
就可以解決問題的。教師
必須知道兒童是如何發
展，並且要放棄所有先入
為主的觀念。要想了解兒
童的心智，需要機智與細

心，但是成人很少具備足夠的條件。很幸運地，兒童從環境中所學習
的，比從我們身上所學習的還要多，但是教師仍需要心理學的見識，才
能盡我們所能去幫助兒童，所以教師必須隨時成長，為發揮自己的潛能
而不斷努力。為了達成這個目標，教師必須真正了解這個需求，而且懂
得如何客觀地反省自己的能力與行為。

Therefore, all teachers must receive certain training since logic alone cannot solve
problems. Teachers must know how the children develop and give up all premeditated

ideas. To understand the minds of
children, one must be attentive and
ingenious. Adults rarely possess
such qualities in sufficient measure.
Fortunately, children learn more
from their surrounding environment
than they do from adults. However,
teachers need to know some

psychology in order to help children. Therefore, teachers must continue learning and
growing at all times and constantly strive to develop their own potential. To do that,
teachers should first understand the need and then be able to objectively examine their
own abilities and conduct.

法界佛教總會・萬佛聖城
Dharma Realm Buddhist Association &
The City of Ten Thousand Buddhas
4951 Bodhi Way, Ukiah, CA 95482 U.S.A.
Tel: (707) 462-0939   Fax: (707) 462-0949

國際譯經學院 The International Translation Institute
1777 Murchison Drive, Burlingame, CA 94010-4504 U.S.A.
Tel: (650) 692-5912   Fax: (650) 692-5056

法界宗教研究院（柏克萊寺）
Institute for World Religions (at Berkeley Buddhist Monastery)
2304 McKinley Avenue, Berkeley, CA 94703 U.S.A.
Tel: (510) 848-3440   Fax: (510) 548-4551

金山聖寺 Gold Mountain Monastery
800 Sacramento Street, San Francisco, CA 94108 U.S.A.
Tel: (415) 421-6117   Fax: (415) 788-6001

金聖寺 Gold Sage Monastery
11455 Clayton Road, San Jose, CA 95127 U.S.A.
Tel: (408) 923-7243   Fax: (408) 923-1064

法界聖城 The City of the Dharma Realm
1029 West Capitol Avenue, West Sacramento, CA 95691 U.S.A.
Tel/Fax: (916) 374-8268

金輪聖寺 Gold Wheel Monastery
235 North Avenue 58, Los Angeles, CA 90042 U.S.A.
Tel/Fax: (323) 258-6668

長堤聖寺 Long Beach Monastery
3361 East Ocean Boulevard, Long Beach, CA 90803 U.S.A.
Tel/Fax: (562) 438-8902

福祿壽聖寺 Blessings,Prosperity, and Longevity Monastery
4140 Long Beach Boulevard, Long Beach, CA 90807 U.S.A.
Tel/Fax: (562) 595-4966

華嚴精舍 Avatamsaka Vihara
9601 Seven Locks Road,
Bethesda, MD 20817-9997 USA
Tel/Fax: (301) 469-8300

金峰聖寺 Gold Summit Monastery
233 First Avenue West, Seattle, WA 98119 U.S.A.
Tel/Fax: (206) 284-6690

金佛聖寺 Gold Buddha Monastery
248 E. 11th Avenue, Vancouver, B.C. V5T 2C3 Canada
Tel: (604) 709-0248   Fax: (604) 684-3754

華嚴聖寺 Avatamsaka Monastery
1009 Fourth Avenue S.W., Calgary, AB T2P 0K8 Canada
Tel/Fax: (403) 234-0644

美國法界佛教總會駐華辦事處（法界佛教印經會）
Dharma Realm Buddhist Books Distribution Society
臺灣省臺北市忠孝東路六段 85 號 11 樓
11th Floor, 85 Chung-Hsiao E. Road, Sec. 6, Taipei, R.O.C.
Tel: (02) 2786-3022, 2786-2474 Fax: (02) 2786-2674

法界聖寺 Dharma Realm Sage Monastery
臺灣省高雄縣六龜鄉興龍村東溪山莊 20 號
20, Tung-hsi Shan-chuang, Hsing-lung Village, Liu-Kuei, Kaohsiung County, Taiwan, R.O.C.
Tel: (07) 689-3713   Fax: (07) 689-3870

彌陀聖寺 Amitabha Monastery
臺灣省花蓮縣壽豐鄉池南村四健會 7 號
7, Su-chien-hui, Chih-nan Village, Shou-Feng, Hualien County, Taiwan, R.O.C.
Tel: (03) 865-1956   Fax:(03) 865-3426

般若觀音聖寺（紫雲洞）
Prajna Guan Yin Sagely Monastery (Tze Yun Tung Temple)
Batu 5 1/2, Jalan Sungai Besi, Salak Selatan, 57100 Kuala Lumpur, Malaysia
Tel: (03) 7982-6560   Fax: (03) 7980-1272

法界觀音聖寺（登彼岸）
Dharma Realm Guanyin Sagely Monastery
(Formerly Deng Bi An Temple)
161, Jalan Ampang, 50450 Kuala Lumpur, Malaysia
Tel: (03) 2164-8055 Fax: (03) 2163-7118

蓮華精舍 Lotus Vihara
136, Jalan Sekolah, 45600 Batang Berjuntai, Selangor Darul Ehsan, Malaysia
Tel: (03) 3271-9439

佛教講堂 Buddhist Lecture Hall
香港跑馬地黃泥涌道 31 號 12 樓
31 Wong Nei Chong Road, Top Floor, Happy Valley, Hong Kong, China
Tel: 2572-7644   Fax: 2572-2850

弟ㄉㄧˋ子ㄗˇ規ㄍㄨㄟ

西曆 2010 年 4 月 29 日‧育良叢書 ICE003

佛曆 3037 年 3 月 16 日‧宣公上人誕辰　恭印

發行人　法界佛教總會

出　版　法界佛教總會‧佛經翻譯委員會‧育良小學

地　址　Dharma Realm Buddhist Association &

　　　　The City of Ten Thousand Buddhas (萬佛聖城)

　　　　P.O. Box 217

　　　　4951 Bodhi Way, Ukiah, CA 95482 U.S.A.

　　　　Tel: (707) 462-0939　　Fax: (707) 462-0949

倡　印　法界佛教印經會

　　　　臺灣省臺北市忠孝東路六段 85 號 11 樓

　　　　Tel: (02) 2786-3022, 2786-2474　Fax: (02) 2786-2674

　　　　劃撥帳號:1321798-5　　帳戶:張淑彤

　　　　法界文教基金會

　　　　臺灣省高雄縣六龜鄉興龍村東溪山莊 20 號

插畫者　梁素霞居士‧林鳴鳳居士

www.drba.org / www.drbachinese.org

13 碼→ISBN 978-0-88139-489-0